Nature's Gifts for baby

From a sparkling pond of water lilies to a splendid sunrise or a playful fox, Nature's gifts make perfect themes for baby blankets and hats.

Coniferous Set 2

Starry Set 7

Fox Set. 10

Seedling Set 15

Sunrise Set 19

Water Lilies Set. 22

Raindrops Set 26

General Instructions 29

Meet Sara Leighton. 31

Yarn Information 32

I0893790

LOOK FOR THE CAMERA in our instructions and watch our technique videos made just for you! **www.LeisureArts.com/6718**

LEISURE ARTS, INC. • Maumelle, Arkansas

Coniferous Set

EASY +

SHOPPING LIST

Yarn (Medium Weight) 4

[7 ounces, 426 yards
(197 grams, 389 meters) per skein]:

- ☐ Green - 1 skein
- ☐ Brown - 1 skein
- ☐ Dk Green - 1 skein
- ☐ Dk Brown - 1 skein

Crochet Hook

- ☐ Size H (5 mm)
  or size needed for gauge

Additional Supplies

- ☐ Yarn needle

SIZE INFORMATION

BLANKET - 37" wide x 30½" long
(94 cm x 77.5 cm)

HAT

Size: 0-6{6-12} Months

Fits Head Circumference:
13-15{16-17}"/33-38{40.5-43} cm

Size Note: We have printed the instructions for the Hat in different colors to make it easier for you to find:

· Size 0-6 Months in Blue

· Size 6-12 Months in Pink

Instructions in Black apply to both sizes.

GAUGE INFORMATION

In Blanket Body pattern,
3 repeats = 5¾" (14.5 cm);
6 rows = 2¾" (7 cm)

Gauge Swatch: 6" wide x 2¾" high
(15.25 cm x 7 cm)

With Green, ch 21.

Work same as Blanket Body Rows 1-6, page 4; at end of Row 6, do **not** change color: 19 dc.

Finish off.

STITCH GUIDE

TREBLE CROCHET
(abbreviated tr)

YO twice, insert hook in st indicated, YO and pull up a loop (4 loops on hook), (YO and draw through 2 loops on hook) 3 times.

SINGLE CROCHET 3 TOGETHER
(abbreviated sc3tog)

Pull up a loop in each of next 3 sts, YO and draw through all 4 loops on hook **(counts as one sc)**.

DOUBLE CROCHET 2 TOGETHER
(abbreviated dc2tog)
(uses next 2 dc)

★ YO, insert hook in **next** dc, YO and pull up a loop, YO and draw through 2 loops on hook; repeat from ★ once **more**, YO and draw through all 3 loops on hook **(counts as one dc)**.

TREBLE CROCHET 2 TOGETHER
(abbreviated tr2tog)
(uses next 2 sc)

★ YO twice, insert hook in **next** sc, YO and pull up a loop, (YO and draw through 2 loops on hook) twice; repeat from ★ once **more**, YO and draw through all 3 loops on hook **(counts as one tr)**.

TREBLE CROCHET 3 TOGETHER
(abbreviated tr3tog)
(uses next 3 sc)

★ YO twice, insert hook in **next** sc, YO and pull up a loop, (YO and draw through 2 loops on hook) twice; repeat from ★ 2 times **more**, YO and draw through all 4 loops on hook **(counts as one tr)**.

MY DAD
IS GREAT

BLANKET

STRIPE SEQUENCE

2 Rows **each** of Green, ★ Brown, Dk Green, Dk Brown, Green; repeat from ★ throughout.

BODY

With Green, ch 117; place marker in third ch from hook for Edging placement.

Row 1 (Right side)**:** Dc in fourth ch from hook **(3 skipped chs count as first dc)** and in each ch across: 115 dc.

Note: Loop a short piece of yarn around any stitch to mark Row 1 as **right** side.

Row 2: Ch 1, turn; sc in first dc, ★ hdc in next dc, dc in next dc, 3 tr in next dc, dc in next dc, hdc in next dc, sc in next dc; repeat from ★ across changing to next color in last sc made ***(Fig. 5a, page 31)***: 153 sts.

Row 3: Ch 1, turn; skip first sc, sc in next 3 sts, 3 sc in next tr, ★ sc in next 2 sts, sc3tog, sc in next 2 sts, 3 sc in next tr; repeat from ★ across to last 4 sts, sc in next 2 sts, skip next hdc, sc in last sc.

Row 4: Ch 1, turn; skip first sc, sc in next 3 sc, 3 sc in next sc, sc in next 2 sc, ★ sc3tog, sc in next 2 sc, 3 sc in next sc, sc in next 2 sc; repeat from ★ across to last 2 sc, skip next sc, sc in last sc changing to next color.

Row 5: Ch 3 **(does not count as a st)**, turn; skip first sc, tr in next sc, dc in next sc, hdc in next sc, sc in next sc, hdc in next sc, dc in next sc, ★ tr3tog, dc in next sc, hdc in next sc, sc in next sc, hdc in next sc, dc in next sc; repeat from ★ across to last 2 sc, tr2tog: 115 sts.

Row 6: Ch 3 **(counts as first dc)**, turn; dc in next dc and in each st across changing to next color in last dc made ***(Fig. 5c, page 31)***.

Row 7: Ch 3 **(counts as first dc)**, turn; dc in next dc and in each dc across.

Rows 8-65: Repeat Rows 2-7, 9 times; then repeat Rows 2-5 once **more**.

Row 66: Ch 3 **(counts as first dc)**, turn; dc in next dc and in each st across changing to Brown in last dc made.

EDGING

Rnd 1: Ch 1, turn; sc in each dc across, ch 1; sc evenly across ends of rows, ch 1; working in free loops of beginning ch ***(Fig. 3, page 30)***, sc in each ch across ending in marked ch, ch 1; sc evenly across ends of rows, ch 1; join with slip st to first sc.

Rnd 2: Ch 1, do **not** turn; sc in same st as joining and in each sc and each corner ch-1 sp around; join with slip st to first sc, finish off.

LARGE TREE

With Dk Green, ch 24.

Row 1 (Right side)**:** Dc in fourth ch from hook **(3 skipped chs do not count as a st)** and in each ch across: 21 dc.

Note: Mark Row 1 as **right** side.

Rows 2-20: Ch 3 **(does not count as a st)**, turn; skip first dc, dc in next dc and in each dc across: 2 dc.

Finish off leaving a long end for sewing.

TRUNK

With Dk Brown, ch 9.

Row 1 (Right side)**:** Dc in fourth ch from hook **(3 skipped chs count as first dc)** and in each ch across: 7 dc.

Note: Mark Row 1 as **right** side.

Rows 2 and 3: Ch 3 **(counts as first dc)**, turn; dc in next dc and in each dc across.

Finish off leaving a long end for sewing.

SMALL TREE

With Green, ch 19.

Row 1 (Wrong side)**:** Dc in fourth ch from hook **(3 skipped chs do not count as a st)** and in each ch across: 16 dc.

Note: Mark the **back** of any stitch on Row 1 to mark **right** side.

Rows 2-15: Ch 3 **(does not count as a st)**, turn; skip first dc, dc in next dc and in each dc across: 2 dc.

Finish off leaving a long end for sewing.

TRUNK

With Dk Brown, ch 7.

Row 1 (Right side)**:** Dc in fourth ch from hook **(3 skipped chs count as first dc)** and in each ch across: 5 dc.

Note: Mark Row 1 as **right** side.

Row 2: Ch 3 **(counts as first dc)**, turn; dc in next dc and in each dc across; finish off leaving a long end for sewing.

Using photo as a guide for placement, sew **wrong** side of Trees and Trunks to **right** side of Blanket.

HAT

With Brown, ch 72{80}; being careful **not** to twist ch, join with slip st to form a ring.

Rnd 1 (Right side)**:** Ch 3 **(counts as first dc, now and throughout)**, dc in next ch, ch 2, skip next 2 chs, ★ dc in next 2 chs, ch 2, skip next 2 chs; repeat from ★ around; join with slip st to first dc: 36{40} dc and 18{20} ch-2 sps.

Rnd 2 (Scale rnd)**:** To form Scale, work 5 dc down post of first dc, ch 1, rotate piece and work 5 dc up post of next dc **(Scale made)**, skip next 2 dc, ***(Figs. A-D)***, ★ work 5 dc down post of next dc, ch 1, rotate piece and work 5 dc up post of next dc, skip next 2 dc; repeat from ★ around; join with slip st to first dc on first Scale: 9{10} Scales.

Fig. A

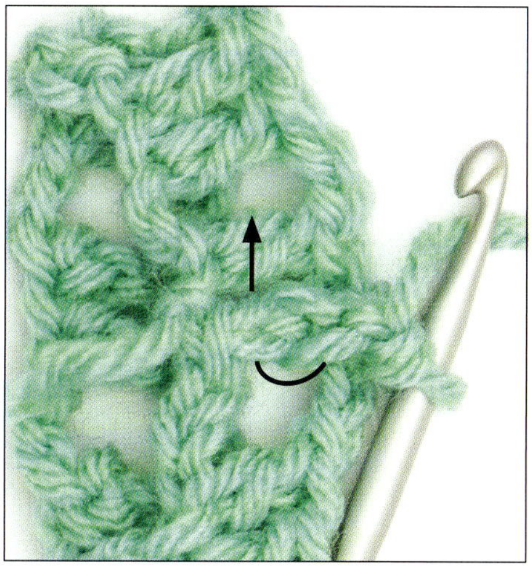

Fig. B

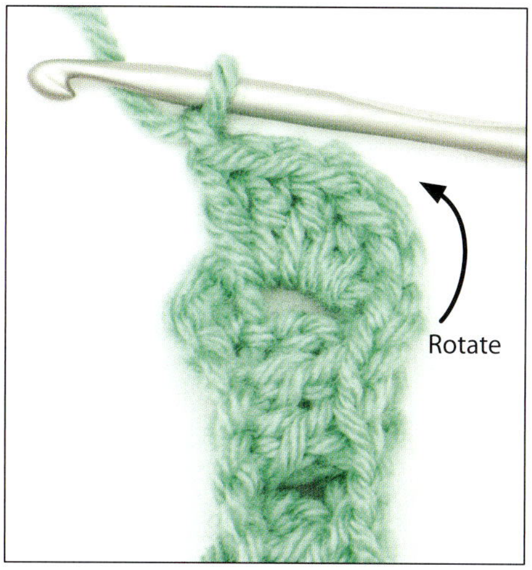

Fig. C

Fig. D

Rnd 3: Ch 3, working **around** previous rnd, dc in sp **between** next 2-dc group on rnd **below** (**before first Scale**) ***(Fig. E)***, ch 2, 2 dc in center of next Scale ***(Fig. F)***, ch 2, ★ working **around** previous rnd, 2 dc in sp **between** next 2-dc group on rnd **below**, ch 2, 2 dc in center of next Scale, ch 2; repeat from ★ around; join with slip st to first dc: 36{40} dc and 18{20} ch-2 sps.

Fig. E

Fig. F

Rnd 4 (Scale rnd)**:** Work 5 dc down post of first dc, ch 1, rotate piece and work 5 dc up post of next dc to form a Scale, skip next 2 dc, ★ work 5 dc down post of next dc, ch 1, rotate piece and work 5 dc up post of next dc, skip next 2 dc; repeat from ★ around; join with slip st to first dc: 9{10} Scales.

Rnds 5-8: Repeat Rnds 3 and 4 twice: 9{10} Scales.

Rnd 9: Ch 3, working **around** previous rnd, dc in sp **between** next 2-dc group on rnd **below**, ch 1, 2 dc in center of next Scale, ch 1, ★ working **around** previous rnd, 2 dc in sp **between** next 2-dc group on rnd **below**, ch 1, 2 dc in center of next Scale, ch 1; repeat from ★ around; join with slip st to first dc: 36{40} dc and 18{20} ch-1 sps.

Rnd 10 (Scale rnd)**:** Work 4 dc down post of first dc, ch 1, rotate piece and work 4 dc up post of next dc to form a Scale, skip next 2 dc, ★ work 4 dc down post of next dc, ch 1, rotate piece and work 4 dc up post of next dc, skip next 2 dc; repeat from ★ around; join with slip st to first dc: 9{10} Scales.

Rnds 11 and 12: Repeat Rnds 9 and 10: 9{10} Scales.

Rnd 13: Ch 3, working **around** previous rnd, dc in sp **between** next 2-dc group on rnd **below**, 2 dc in center of next Scale, ★ working **around** previous rnd, 2 dc in sp **between** next 2-dc group on rnd **below**, 2 dc in center of next Scale; repeat from ★ around; join with slip st to first dc: 36{40} dc.

SIZE 0-6 MONTHS ONLY

Rnd 14: Ch 2 (**does not count as a st**), (dc in next 3 dc, dc2tog) around; skip beginning ch-2 and join with slip st to first dc: 28 dc.

SIZE 6-12 MONTHS ONLY

Rnd 14: Ch 3, dc in next 2 dc, dc2tog, (dc in next 3 dc, dc2tog) around; join with slip st to first dc: 32 dc.

BOTH SIZES

Rnds 15 and 16: Ch 2 (**does not count as a st**), dc in next dc, dc2tog around; skip beginning ch-2 and join with slip st to first dc: 7{8} dc.

Stem: Ch 4, hdc in second ch from hook, sc in last 2 chs, skip next 2 dc, slip st in next dc, leave remaining dc unworked; finish off.

Starry Set

EASY

SHOPPING LIST

Yarn (Medium Weight) MEDIUM 4

[5 ounces, 256 yards (141 grams, 234 meters) per skein]:

- ☐ Navy - 5 skeins
- ☐ Off White - 1 skein

Crochet Hook

- ☐ Size I (5.5 mm) **or** size needed for gauge

Additional Supplies

- ☐ Yarn needle

SIZE INFORMATION

BLANKET - 38¼" wide x 26½" long (97 cm x 67.5 cm)

HAT

Size: 0-6{6-12} Months

Fits Head Circumference: 13-15{16-17}"/33-38{40.5-43} cm

Size Note: We have printed the instructions for the Hat in different colors to make it easier for you to find:

· Size 0-6 Months in Blue

· Size 6-12 Months in Pink

Instructions in Black apply to both sizes.

GAUGE INFORMATION

Blanket - 16 sc and 19 rows = 4" (10 cm)

Hat - Rnds 1 and 2 = 2" (5 cm)

Gauge Swatch: 4" (10 cm) square

With Blue, ch 17.

Row 1: Sc in second ch from hook and in each ch across: 16 sc.

Rows 2-19: Ch 1, turn; sc in each sc across.

Finish off.

BLANKET

BODY

With Navy, ch 150; place marker in second ch from hook for Edging placement.

Row 1 (Wrong side)**:** Sc in second ch from hook and in each ch across: 149 sc.

Note: Loop a short piece of yarn around the **back** of any stitch on Row 1 to mark **right** side.

Rows 2-122: Ch 1, turn; sc in each sc across.

Finish off.

EDGING

Rnd 1: With **right** side facing and working in sc across Row 122, join Off White with sc in first sc ***(see Joining With Sc, page 30)***; skip next sc, sc in each sc across, ch 2; skip first row, sc in end of each row across, ch 2; working in free loops of beginning ch ***(Fig. 3, page 30)***, sc in marked ch, skip next ch, sc in each ch across, ch 2; skip first row, sc in end of each row across, ch 1, sc in first sc to form last ch-2 sp; join with slip st to first sc: 538 sc and 4 ch-2 sps.

Rnd 2: Ch 1, sc in last ch-2 sp made, ★ † (sc, ch 3, sc) in next sc, ♥ sc in next sc, skip next sc, (sc, ch 3, sc) in next sc ♥; repeat from ♥ to ♥ across to next corner ch-2 sp †, sc in corner ch-2 sp; repeat from ★ 2 times **more**, then repeat from † to † once; join with slip st to first sc, finish off.

DIAGRAM

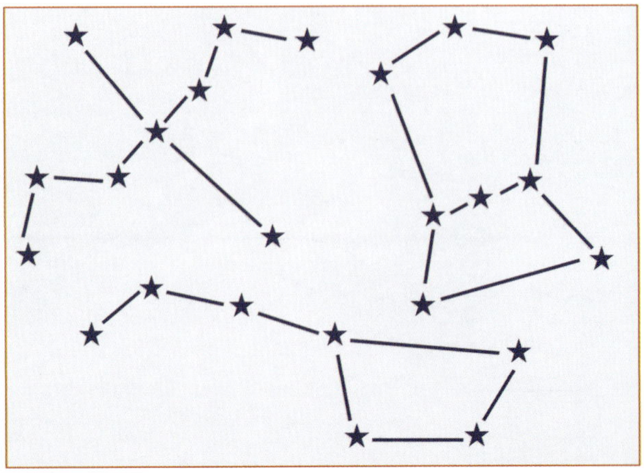

STAR (Make 24)

With Off White, ch 6.

Rnd 1: Sc in sixth ch from hook, ch 4, (sc in same ch as first sc, ch 4) 3 times, slip st in same ch as first sc; finish off leaving a long for sewing: 5 sps.

Using Diagram for placement and long end, sew Stars to **right** side of Body.

ACCENT LINES

Surface slip stitch is worked on the **right** side of crocheted fabric using Diagram, page 8, as a guide for placement. The slip stitches will create lines to connect the stars, while the working yarn is held continuously on the **wrong** side.

To work surface slip st, make a slip knot with Off White. With the **right** side of the Body facing and slip knot on **wrong** side, insert the hook from the **right** side to the **wrong** side in stitch ½" (12 mm) from any star and place the loop of the slip knot on hook; pull the loop through to the **right** side. ★ Insert your hook from the **right** side to the **wrong** side ***(Fig. A)***, YO and pull loop through the piece **and** the loop on the hook; repeat from ★ across to ½" (12 mm) from next star.

Fig. A

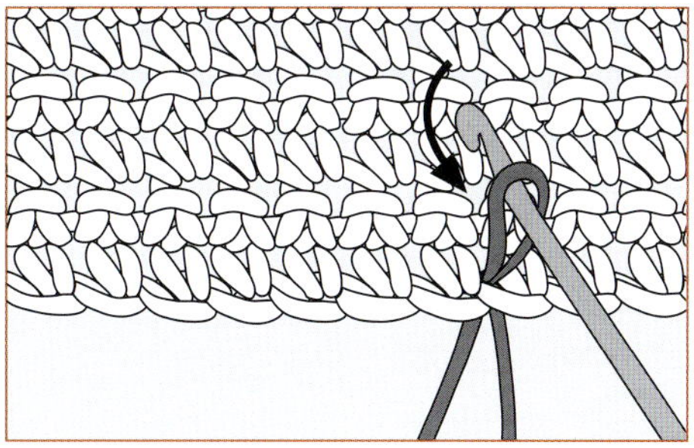

At the end of an accent line, cut yarn and pull the yarn to the **right** side through the last slip st made. To secure the last loop, thread the yarn needle with the end and insert it back through the fabric on the outside of the loop, pull yarn to the **wrong** side; secure end.

Repeat for remaining accent lines.

HAT

With Navy, ch 4.

Rnd 1 (Right side)**:** 10 Dc in fourth ch from hook; skip beginning ch and join with slip st to first dc: 10 dc.

Rnd 2: Ch 3 **(does not count as a st, now and throughout)**, 2 dc in same st as joining and in each dc around; skip beginning ch-3 **(now and throughout)** and join with slip st to first dc: 20 dc.

Rnd 3: Ch 3, dc in same st as joining, 2 dc in next dc, (dc in next dc, 2 dc in next dc) around; join with slip st to first dc: 30 dc.

Rnd 4: Ch 3, dc in same st as joining and in next dc, 2 dc in next dc, (dc in next 2 dc, 2 dc in next dc) around; join with slip st to first dc: 40 dc.

Rnd 5: Ch 3, dc in same st as joining and in next 2 dc, 2 dc in next dc, (dc in next 3 dc, 2 dc in next dc) around; join with slip st to first dc: 50 dc.

Rnd 6: Ch 3, dc in same st as joining and in next 3 dc, 2 dc in next dc, (dc in next 4 dc, 2 dc in next dc) around; join with slip st to first dc: 60 dc.

SIZE 6-12 MONTHS ONLY

Rnd 7: Ch 3, dc in same st as joining and in next 3 dc, 2 dc in next dc, (dc in next 4 dc, 2 dc in next dc) around; join with slip st to first dc: 72 dc.

BOTH SIZES

Last 4 Rnds: Ch 3, dc in same st as joining and in each dc around; join with slip st to first dc.

Finish off.

Trim: With **right** side facing, join Off White with sc in same st as joining ***(see Joining With Sc, page 30)***; ch 3, sc in same st, sc in next dc, skip next dc, ★ (sc, ch 3, sc) in next dc, sc in next dc, skip next dc; repeat from ★ around; join with slip st to first sc, finish off.

Make one Star.

Using photo as guide for placement and long end, sew Star to Hat.

Fox Set

EASY

SHOPPING LIST

Yarn (Super Bulky Weight) SUPER BULKY 6

[5 ounces, 87 yards
(140 grams, 80 meters) per skein]:

- ☐ Brown - 3 skeins

[6 ounces, 106 yards
(170 grams, 97 meters) per skein]:

- ☐ Beige - 3 skeins
- ☐ Orange - 2 skeins

Crochet Hook

- ☐ Size M/N (9 mm)
  or size needed for gauge

Additional Supplies

- ☐ Yarn needle

SIZE INFORMATION

BLANKET - 30½" wide x 34½" long (77.5 cm x 87.5 cm)

HAT

Size: 0-6{6-12} Months

Fits Head Circumference:
13-15{16-17}"/33-38{40.5-43} cm

Size Note: We have printed the instructions for the Hat in different colors to make it easier for you to find:

- Size 0-6 Months in Blue
- Size 6-12 Months in Pink

Instructions in Black apply to both sizes.

GAUGE INFORMATION

Blanket - 8 hdc and 7 rows/rnds = 4" (10 cm)

Hat - Rnds 1 and 2 = 2¼" (5.75 cm)

Gauge Swatch: 4" (10 cm) square

With Beige, ch 9.

Row 1: Hdc in third ch from hook (**2 skipped chs count as first hdc**) and in each ch across: 8 hdc.

Rows 2-7: Ch 2 (**counts as first hdc**), turn; hdc in next hdc and in each hdc across.

Finish off.

STITCH GUIDE

SINGLE CROCHET 2 TOGETHER ***(abbreviated sc2tog)***

Pull up a loop in each of next 2 sc, YO and draw through all 3 loops on hook (**counts as one sc**).

BLANKET

Each row is worked across the length of the Body.

BODY

With Beige, ch 67; place marker in second ch from hook for Edging placement.

Row 1 (Right side)**:** Hdc in third ch from hook (**2 skipped chs count as first hdc**) and in each ch across: 66 hdc.

Note: Loop a short piece of yarn around any stitch to mark Row 1 as **right** side.

Rows 2-4: Ch 2 (**counts as first hdc, now and throughout**), turn; hdc in next hdc and in each hdc across.

Row 5: Ch 2, turn; hdc in next hdc and in each hdc across changing to Brown in last hdc made *(Fig. 5b, page 31)*; cut Beige.

Rows 6-12: Ch 2, turn; hdc in next hdc and in each hdc across.

Row 13: Ch 2, turn; hdc in next hdc and in each hdc across changing to Beige in last hdc made; cut Brown.

Rows 14-16: Ch 2, turn; hdc in next hdc and in each hdc across.

Row 17: Ch 2, turn; hdc in next hdc and in each hdc across changing to Brown in last hdc made; cut Beige.

Rows 18-20: Ch 2, turn; hdc in next hdc and in each hdc across.

Row 21: Ch 2, turn; hdc in next hdc and in each hdc across changing to Beige in last hdc made; cut Brown.

Rows 22-32: Ch 2, turn; hdc in next hdc and in each hdc across.

Row 33: Ch 2, turn; hdc in next hdc and in each hdc across changing to Brown in last hdc made; cut Beige.

Rows 34-42: Ch 2, turn; hdc in next hdc and in each hdc across.

Row 43: Ch 2, turn; hdc in next hdc and in each hdc across changing to Beige in last hdc made; cut Brown.

Rows 44-50: Ch 2, turn; hdc in next hdc and in each hdc across.

Row 51: Ch 2, turn; hdc in next hdc and in each hdc across changing to Brown in last hdc made; cut Beige.

EDGING

Rnd 1: Ch 1, do **not** turn; sc in end of each row across, ch 2; working in free loops of beginning ch *(Fig. 3, page 30)*, sc in each ch across ending in marked ch, ch 2; sc in end of each row across, ch 2; working in hdc across Row 51, sc in each hdc across, ch 2; join with slip st to first sc, finish off: 234 sc and 4 ch-2 sps.

Rnd 2: With **right** side facing, join Orange with sc in same st as joining *(see Joining With Sc, page 30)*; ★ sc in each sc across to next corner ch-2 sp, 3 sc in ch-2 sp; repeat from ★ around; join with slip st to first sc, finish off.

FOX

BODY

With Orange, ch 11.

Row 1 (Right side)**:** Sc in second ch from hook and in each ch across: 10 sc.

Note: Mark Row 1 as **right** side.

Row 2: Ch 1, turn; 2 sc in first sc, sc in next 8 sc, 2 sc in last sc: 12 sc.

Rows 3-6: Ch 1, turn; sc in each sc across.

Row 7: Ch 1, turn; beginning in first sc, sc2tog, sc in next 8 sc, sc2tog: 10 sc.

Rows 8-10: Ch 1, turn; sc in each sc across.

Rows 11 and 12: Ch 1, turn; beginning in first sc, sc2tog, sc in each sc across to last 2 sc, sc2tog: 6 sc.

Rows 13 and 14: Ch 1, turn; sc in each sc across.

Row 15: Ch 1, turn; beginning in first sc, sc2tog, sc in next 2 sc, sc2tog; finish off leaving a long end for sewing: 4 sc.

HEAD

With Orange, ch 10.

Row 1 (Right side)**:** Sc in second ch from hook and in each ch across: 9 sc.

Note: Mark Row 1 as **right** side.

Rows 2 and 3: Ch 1, turn; sc in each sc across.

Rows 4 and 5: Ch 1, turn; skip first sc, sc in each sc across: 7 sc.

Row 6: Ch 1, turn; skip first sc, sc in next 5 sc, leave remaining sc unworked: 5 sc.

Rows 7 and 8: Ch 1, turn; sc in each sc across.

Row 9: Ch 1, turn; skip first sc, sc in next 3 sc changing to Brown in last sc made *(Fig. 5a, page 31)*, leave remaining sc unworked; cut Orange: 3 sc.

Nose

Row 1: Ch 1, turn; sc in each sc across.

Row 2: Ch 1, turn; skip first sc, sc in last 2 sc: 2 sc.

Row 3: Ch 1, turn; skip first sc, sc in last sc; finish off: one sc.

First Ear

Row 1: With **right** side of Head facing and working in free loops of beginning ch, join Brown with sc in first ch; sc in next 2 chs, leave remaining chs unworked: 3 sc.

Row 2: Ch 1, turn; skip first sc, sc in last 2 sc: 2 sc.

Row 3: Ch 1, turn; skip first sc, sc in last sc; finish off: one sc.

Second Ear

Row 1: With **right** side of Head facing and working in free loops of beginning ch, skip next 3 chs from last sc on First Ear and join Brown with sc in next ch; sc in next 2 chs: 3 sc.

Beginning with Row 2, complete same as First Ear.

Eyelids

With Brown, make a slip knot. Using photo as a guide for placement, page 11, and holding Brown to **wrong** side of Row 3 on Head, insert hook from **right** side in sc, hook loop and pull through st; (slip st in next sc) twice to form Eyelid; finish off.

Repeat for second Eyelid.

Cheeks

Thread yarn needle with Beige. Using photo, page 11, as a guide for placement, work overcast stitches around ends of rows as follows: Insert needle from **back** to **front** around end of Row 9, pull needle through; continue in this manner, working stitches close to each other until you reach Row 5; cut yarn.

Repeat on opposite side beginning at Row 5 and ending at Row 9.

TAIL

With Orange, ch 6.

Row 1: Sc in second ch from hook and in each ch across: 5 sc.

Row 2 (Right side): Ch 1, turn; 2 sc in first sc, sc in next 3 sc, 2 sc in last sc: 7 sc.

Row 3: Ch 1, turn; sc in each sc across.

Row 4: Ch 1, turn; 2 sc in first sc, sc in next 5 sc, 2 sc in last sc: 9 sc.

Rows 5 and 6: Ch 1, turn; beginning in first sc, sc2tog, sc in each sc across to last 2 sc, sc2tog: 5 sc.

Row 7: Ch 1, turn; sc in each sc across.

Row 8: Ch 1, turn; sc in each sc across changing to Beige in last sc made.

Row 9: Ch 1, turn; beginning in first sc, sc2tog, sc in next sc, sc2tog: 3 sc.

Row 10: Ch 1, turn; skip first sc, sc in last 2 sc: 2 sc.

Row 11: Ch 1, turn; skip first sc, sc in last sc; finish off leaving a long end for sewing: one sc.

Using photo, page 11, as a guide for placement:
Sew **wrong** side of Tail to **right** side of bottom of Blanket.
Sew **wrong** side of Body to **right** side of Blanket overlapping the Tail.
Sew **wrong** side of Head to **right** side of Blanket overlapping the Body.

HAT

BODY

With Orange, ch 3; join with slip st to form a ring.

Rnd 1 (Right side)**:** Ch 2 (**does not count as a st, now and throughout**), 8 hdc in ring; skip begining ch-2 (**now and throughout**) and join with slip st to first hdc.

Rnd 2: Ch 2, 2 hdc in same st as joining and in each hdc around; join with slip st to first hdc: 16 hdc.

Rnd 3: Ch 2, hdc in same st as joining, 2 hdc in next hdc, (hdc in next hdc, 2 hdc in next hdc) around; join with slip st to first hdc: 24 hdc.

Rnd 4: Ch 2, hdc in same st as joining and in next hdc, 2 hdc in next hdc, (hdc in next 2 hdc, 2 hdc in next hdc) around; join with slip st to first hdc: 32 hdc.

SIZE 6-12 MONTHS ONLY

Rnd 5: Ch 2, hdc in same st as joining and in next 3 hdc, 2 hdc in next hdc, (hdc in next 4 hdc, 2 hdc in next hdc) around to last 2 hdc, hdc in last 2 hdc; join with slip st to first hdc: 38 hdc.

BOTH SIZES

Last 4 Rnds: Ch 2, hdc in same st as joining and in each hdc around; join with slip st to first hdc.

Finish off.

EAR (Make 2)

INNER EAR

With Beige, ch 6.

Row 1 (Right side)**:** Sc in second ch from hook and in each ch across: 5 sc.

Note: Mark Row 1 as **right** side.

Row 2: Ch 1, turn; sc in each sc across.

Rows 3-5: Ch 1, turn; skip first sc, sc in each sc across: 2 sc.

Row 6: Ch 1, turn; skip first sc, sc in last sc; finish off: one sc.

OUTER EAR

With Brown, work same as Inner Ear; finish off leaving a long end for sewing.

Thread yarn needle with long end. With **wrong** sides together; sew Inner and Outer Ears together.

Using photo as a guide for placement, sew each Ear to Hat.

Seedling Set

EASY +

SHOPPING LIST

Yarn (Medium Weight) 4

[7 ounces, 370 yards (198 grams, 338 meters) per skein]:

- ☐ Aran - 2 skeins
- ☐ Brown - 1 skein
- ☐ Green - 1 skein

Crochet Hook

- ☐ Size J (6 mm) **or** size needed for gauge

Additional Supplies

- ☐ Yarn needle

SIZE INFORMATION

BLANKET - 29" wide x 36½" long (73.5 cm x 92.5 cm)

HAT

Size: 0-6{6-12} Months

Fits Head Circumference: 13-15{16-17}"/33-38{40.5-43} cm

Size Note: We have printed the instructions for the Hat in different colors to make it easier for you to find:

· Size 0-6 Months in Blue

· Size 6-12 Months in Pink

Instructions in Black apply to both sizes.

GAUGE INFORMATION

Blanket - 14 hdc and 11 rows = 4" (10 cm)

Each Blanket Block = 14" wide x 17¾" high (35.5 cm x 45 cm)

Hat - Rnds 1 and 2 = 2½" (6.25 cm)

Gauge Swatch: 4" (10 cm) square

With Aran, ch 16.

Row 1 (Right side)**:** Hdc in third ch from hook **(2 skipped chs does not count as a st)** and in each ch across: 14 hdc.

Rows 2-11: Ch 2 **(does not count as a st)**, hdc in first hdc and in each hdc across.

Finish off.

BLANKET

SEED BLOCK

With Aran, ch 47; place marker in third ch from hook for Edging placement.

Row 1 (Right side)**:** Hdc in third ch from hook **(2 skipped chs do not count as a st, now and throughout)** and in each ch across: 45 hdc.

Note: Loop a short piece of yarn around any stitch to mark Row 1 as **right** side.

Row 2: Ch 2 **(does not count as a st, now and throughout)**, turn; hdc in first 10 hdc, hdc in next hdc changing to Brown in last hdc made *(Fig. A)*, hdc in next 3 hdc, hdc in next hdc changing to Aran, hdc in next hdc and in each hdc across.

Fig. A

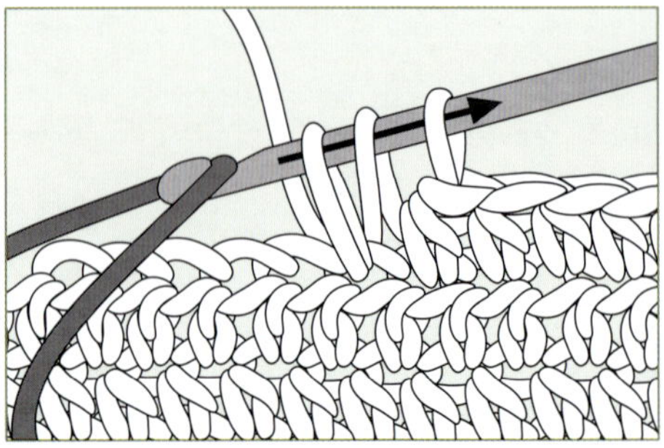

Carry the unused color **loosely** on the **wrong** side and work over the carried yarn on subsequent rows *(Fig. B)*. Cut yarns when no longer needed.

Fig. B

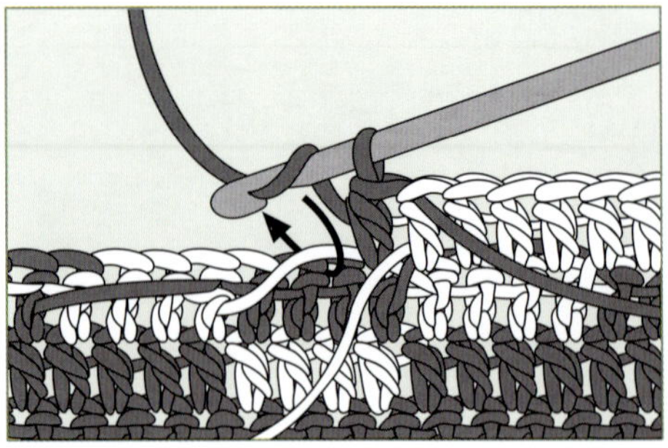

Rows 3-45: Ch 2, turn; hdc in next hdc and in each hdc across following Chart A Rows 3-45 *(see How to Follow a Chart, page 18)*; at end of Row 45, do **not** finish off Aran, cut Green.

EDGING

Rnd 1: With Aran, ch 2, do **not** turn; † working in ends of rows, 2 hdc in first row, (hdc in next row, 2 hdc in next row) across, ch 2 †; working in free loops of beginning ch *(Fig. 3, page 30)*, hdc in each ch across ending in marked ch, ch 2; repeat from † to † once; hdc in each hdc across Row 45, ch 2; skip beginning ch-2 and join with slip st to first hdc, finish off: 226 hdc and 4 corner ch-2 sps.

Rnd 2: With **right** side facing, join Brown with hdc in any corner ch-2 sp *(see Joining With Hdc, page 30)*; 2 hdc in same sp, ★ hdc in next hdc and in each hdc across to next corner ch-2 sp, 3 hdc in corner ch-2 sp; repeat from ★ 2 times **more**, hdc in next hdc and in each hdc across; join with slip st to first hdc, finish off: 238 hdc.

REMAINING 3 BLOCKS

With Aran, ch 47; place marker in third ch from hook for Edging placement.

Row 1 (Right side)**:** Hdc in third ch from hook and in each ch across following next chart: 45 hdc.

Rows 2-45: Ch 2, turn; hdc in first hdc and in each hdc across following Rows 2-45 of the chart.

EDGING

Work same as Seed Block.

ASSEMBLY

Using photo, page 15, as a guide for placement, hold 2 bottom Blocks side-by-side with **right** sides facing. Thread yarn needle with Brown and sew Blocks together *(Figs. C & D)*. Join remaining Blocks together in same manner; then join strips together.

Fig. C

Fig. D

BORDER

With **right** side facing, join Green with hdc in center hdc of any 3-hdc group; 2 hdc in same st, hdc in each hdc around working 3 hdc in center hdc of each corner 3-hdc group; join with slip st to first hdc, finish off.

HAT

BODY

With Brown, ch 3; join with slip st to form a ring.

Rnd 1 (Right side)**:** Ch 3 **(does not count as a st, now and throughout)**, 12 dc in ring; skip beginning ch-3 (now and throughout) and join with slip st to first dc.

Rnd 2: Ch 3, 2 dc in same st as joining and in each dc around; join with slip st to first dc: 24 dc.

Rnd 3: Ch 3, dc in same st as joining, 2 dc in next dc, (dc in next dc, 2 dc in next dc) around; join with slip st to first dc: 36 dc.

Rnd 4: Ch 3, dc in same st as joining and in next 2{1} dc, 2 dc in next dc, ★ dc in next 3{2} dc, 2 dc in next dc; repeat from ★ around; join with slip st to first dc: 45{48} dc.

Rnds 5 thru 9{10}: Ch 3, dc in same st as joining and in each dc around; join with slip st to first dc.

Finish off.

SPROUT

With Green, ch 8.

Leaf: Sc in second ch from hook, hdc in next ch, dc in next 3 chs, hdc in next ch, (sc, ch 1, sc) in last ch; working in free loops of beginning ch *(Fig. 3, page 30)*, hdc in next ch, dc in next 3 chs, hdc in next ch, sc in next ch: 15 sts.

Stem: Ch 7, working in back ridge of ch *(Fig. 1, page 30)*, slip st in second ch from hook and in next ch, skip next ch, slip st in next 2 chs, skip last ch, slip st in ch at base of last sc on Leaf; finish off leaving a long end for sewing.

Sew Sprout to top of Hat.

HOW TO FOLLOW A CHART

The chart shows each stitch as a square, indicating what color each stitch should be.

To keep your place, a ruler, piece of paper, or a sticky note can be placed above the row you are working. You need to see the row you have just completed to ensure you are working the correct color.

CHARTS

On **right** side rows, follow the chart from **right** to left.

On **wrong** side rows, follow the chart from **left** to **right**.

Key

- Aran
- Green
- Brown

SEED

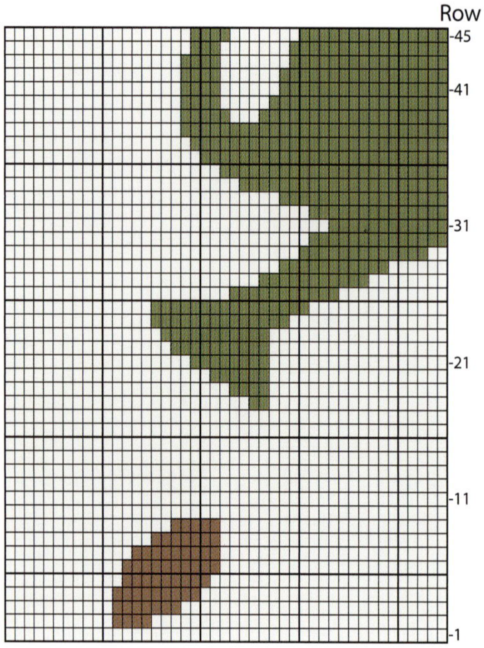

BUD

SPROUT

BLOOM

Sunrise Set

INTERMEDIATE

SHOPPING LIST

Yarn (Medium Weight) MEDIUM 4

[6 ounces, 315 yards

(170.1 grams, 288 meters) per skein]:

- ☐ Red - 2 skeins
- ☐ Orange - 2 skeins
- ☐ Yellow - 1 skein

Crochet Hook

- ☐ Size H (5 mm)

  or size needed for gauge

SIZE INFORMATION

BLANKET - 23½" wide x 32½" long (59.5 cm x 82.5 cm)

HAT

Size: 0-6{6-12} Months

Fits Head Circumference: 13-15{16-17}"/33-38{40.5-43} cm

Size Note: We have printed the instructions for the Hat in different colors to make it easier for you to find:

- Size 0-6 Months in Blue
- Size 6-12 Months in Pink

Instructions in Black apply to both sizes.

GAUGE INFORMATION

Each Hexagon = 3" (7.5 cm) from straight edge to straight edge

Gauge Swatch: 2" (5 cm) diameter

Work same as Hexagon through Rnd 2: 12 Clusters and 12 ch-1 sps.

STITCH GUIDE

TREBLE CROCHET *(abbreviated tr)*

YO twice, insert hook in sp indicated, YO and pull up a loop (4 loops on hook), (YO and draw through 2 loops on hook) 3 times.

CLUSTER (uses one sc)

★ YO, insert hook in sc indicated, YO and pull up a loop, YO and draw through 2 loops on hook; repeat from ★ once **more**, YO and draw through all 3 loops on hook.

BLANKET

HEXAGON (Make 70)

With Yellow, ch 4; join with slip st to form a ring.

Rnd 1 (Right side)**:** Ch 1, 12 sc in ring; join with slip st to first sc.

Note: Loop a short piece of yarn around any stitch to mark Rnd 1 as **right** side.

Rnd 2: Ch 3, dc in same st as joining (**beginning Cluster made**), ch 1, (work Cluster in next sc, ch 1) around; join with slip st to top of beginning Cluster, finish off: 12 Clusters and 12 ch-1 sps.

Rnd 3: With **right** side facing, join Orange with dc in any ch-1 sp ***(see Joining With Dc, page 30)***; ch 1, ★ (dc, tr, dc) in next ch-1 sp, ch 1, dc in next ch-1 sp, ch 1; repeat from ★ around; join with slip st to first dc, finish off: 24 sts and 12 ch-1 sps.

Rnd 4: With **right** side facing, join Red with sc in any tr ***(see Joining With Sc, page 30)***; 2 sc in same st, ★ † sc in next dc, (sc in next ch-1 sp and in next dc) twice †, 3 sc in next tr; repeat from ★ 4 times **more**, then repeat from † to † once; join with slip st to first sc, finish off: 48 sc.

ASSEMBLY

Center sc of 3-sc groups will be worked into more than once.

Work through inside loops only throughout Assembly.

Join Center 2 Hexagons as follows: With **wrong** sides together and working through **both** thicknesses, join Red with sc in center sc of first 3-sc group; sc in next 7 sc, sc in center sc of next 3-sc group; finish off.

The next 8 Hexagons will be joined around the Center Hexagons as follows:

Using Diagram as a guide for placement and beginning at red arrow, hold first Hexagon and Center Hexagon with **wrong** sides together, join Red with sc in center sc of first 3-sc group; sc in next 8 sc; do **not** finish off.

Join second and third Hexagons as follows: With **wrong** sides together and working through **both** thicknesses, sc in center sc of first 3-sc group on new Hexagon **and** in same sc as last sc on Center Hexagon, sc in next 8 sc; do **not** finish off.

Join fourth Hexagon as follows: With **wrong** sides together and working through **both** thicknesses, sc in center sc of first 3-sc group on new Hexagon **and** in same sc as last sc on Center Hexagon, sc in next 7 sc, sc in next center sc on new Hexagon **and** in joined sc on Center Hexagon, sc in same sc on new Hexagon **and** in joined center sc on **next** Center Hexagon, sc in next 8 sc; do **not** finish off.

Joining remaining four Hexagons in same manner; at the end of the last joining, finish off.

Continue joining Hexagons in same manner for the remaining three rounds.

Join the openings between the Hexagons in same manner.

EDGING

With **right** side facing and working in Back Loops Only *(Fig. 2, page 30)*, join Red with sc in any sc; sc in each sc around; join with slip st to first sc, finish off.

HAT

Rnds 1-4: Work same as Hexagon, page 20: 48 sc.

DIAGRAM

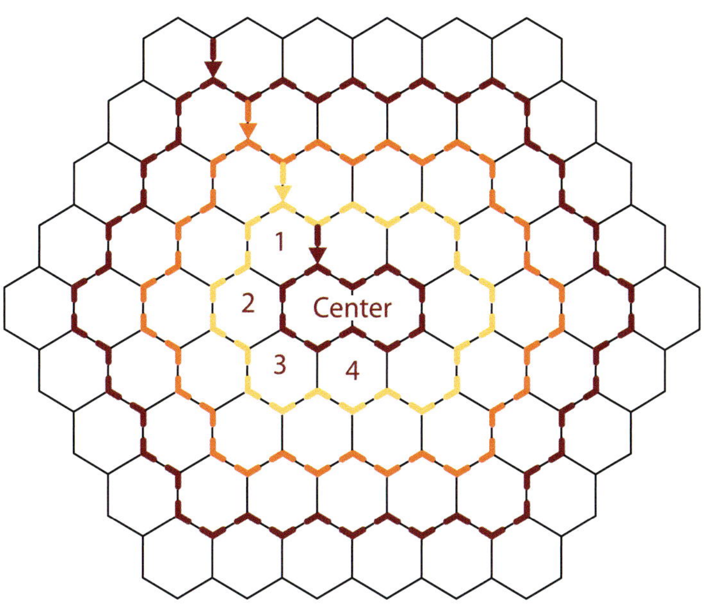

Rnd 5: With **right** side facing, join Yellow with slip st in same st as joining; ch 2 **(does not count as a st, now and throughout)**, dc in same st, 2 dc in next 2 sc, (dc in next 3 sc, 2 dc in next sc) around to last 2 sc, dc in last 2 sc; cut Yellow; skip beginning ch-2 **(now and throughout)** and join with slip st to first dc changing to Orange *(Fig. 5d, page 31)*, finish off: 60 dc.

SIZE 0-6 MONTHS ONLY

Stripe Sequence: One rnd **each** of (Orange, Red, Yellow) twice.

Rnds 6-11: Ch 2, dc in same st as joining and in each dc around changing to next color; join with slip st to first dc; at end of Rnd 11, do **not** change color.

Finish off.

SIZE 6-12 MONTHS ONLY

Rnd 6: Ch 2, dc in same st as joining and in next 8 dc, 2 dc in next dc, (dc in next 9 dc, 2 dc in next dc) around, cut Orange; join with slip st to first dc changing to Red: 66 dc.

Stripe Sequence: One rnd **each** of (Red, Yellow, Orange) twice.

Rnds 7-12: Ch 2, dc in same st as joining and in each dc around changing to next color; join with slip st to first dc; at end of Rnd 12, do **not** change color.

Finish off.

Water Lilies Set

EASY

SHOPPING LIST

Yarn (Medium Weight) 4

[4 ounces, 204 yards
(113 grams, 186 meters) per skein]:

- ☐ Teal Ombre - 5 skeins
- ☐ Green Ombre - 1 skein
- ☐ Rose Ombre - 1 skein

Crochet Hook

- ☐ Size I (5.5 mm)
  or size needed for gauge

Additional Supplies

- ☐ Yarn needle

SIZE INFORMATION

BLANKET - 31½" wide x 23½" long (80 cm x 59.5 cm)

HAT

Size: 0-6{6-12} Months

Fits Head Circumference:
13-15{16-17}"/33-38{40.5-43} cm

Size Note: We have printed the instructions for the Hat in different colors to make it easier for you to find:

- Size 0-6 Months in Blue
- Size 6-12 Months in Pink

Instructions in Black apply to both sizes.

GAUGE INFORMATION

Blanket - In pattern, one repeat (14 sts) and 11 rows = 3" (7.5 cm)

Hat - Rnds 1 and 2 = 2" (5 cm)

Gauge Swatch: 6" wide x 3¼" high (15.25 cm x 8.25 cm)

With Teal Ombre, ch 32.

Work same as Blanket Body for 12 rows: 29 sc.

Finish off.

BLANKET

BODY

With Teal Ombre, ch 144.

Row 1 (Right side)**:** 3 Dc in fourth ch from hook **(3 skipped chs count as first dc)**, skip next 3 chs, sc in next 7 chs, ★ skip next 3 chs, 7 dc in next ch, skip next 3 chs, sc in next 7 chs; repeat from ★ across to last 4 chs, skip next 3 chs, 4 dc in last ch: 141 sts.

Note: Loop a short piece of yarn around any stitch to mark Row 1 as **right** side.

Row 2: Ch 1, turn; sc in each st across.

Row 3: Ch 1, turn; sc in first 4 sc, skip next 3 sc, 7 dc in next sc, ★ skip next 3 sc, sc in next 7 sc, skip next 3 sc, 7 dc in next sc; repeat from ★ across to last 7 sc, skip next 3 sc, sc in last 4 sc.

Row 4: Ch 1, turn; sc in each st across.

Row 5: Ch 3 **(counts as first dc, now and throughout)**, turn; 3 dc in first sc, skip next 3 sc, sc in next 7 sc, ★ skip next 3 sc, 7 dc in next sc, skip next 3 sc, sc in next 7 sc; repeat from ★ across to last 4 sc, skip next 3 sc, 4 dc in last sc.

Rows 6-80: Repeat Rows 2-5, 18 times; then repeat Rows 2-4 once **more**; at end of Row 80, change to Rose Ombre in last sc made *(Fig. 5a, page 31)*.

EDGING

Rnd 1: Ch 2 **(counts as first hdc, now and throughout)**, turn; hdc in next sc and in each sc across, ch 1; working in ends of rows, hdc in first 3 sc rows, 3 hdc in next dc row, (hdc in next 3 sc rows, 3 hdc in next dc row) across, ch 1; working over chs and in free loops of beginning ch ***(Fig. 3, page 30)***, hdc in first ch, ★ 3 hdc in next sp, hdc in next 7 chs, 3 hdc in next sp, hdc in next ch; repeat from ★ across, ch 1; working in ends of rows, 3 hdc in first dc row, (hdc in next 3 sc rows, 3 hdc in next dc row) across; ch 1, cut Teal Ombre; join with slip st to first hdc changing to Green Ombre ***(Fig. 5d, page 31)***: 522 hdc and 4 corner ch-1 sps.

Rnd 2: Ch 2, do **not** turn; 2 hdc in next hdc and in each hdc and each corner ch-1 sp around; join with slip st to first hdc, finish off.

LILY PAD (Make 7)

With Green Ombre, ch 3; join with slip st to form a ring.

Row 1 (Right side)**:** Ch 3, 12 dc in ring; do **not** join: 13 dc.

Note: Mark Row 1 as **right** side.

Row 2: Ch 3, turn; dc in first dc, 2 dc in each of next 5 dc, 3 dc in next dc, 2 dc in each of last 6 dc: 27 dc.

Row 3: Ch 3, turn; dc in first 3 dc, 2 dc in next dc, dc in next dc, hdc in next 4 dc, sc in next 4 dc, 3 hdc in next dc, sc in next 4 dc, hdc in next 4 dc, dc in next dc, 2 dc in next dc, dc in next 2 dc, 2 dc in last dc; finish off leaving a long end for sewing.

LILY (Make 3)

With Rose Ombre, ch 3; join with slip st to form a ring.

Rnd 1 (Right side)**:** Ch 2, 12 dc in ring; join with slip st to first dc: 12 dc.

Note: Mark Rnd 1 as **right** side.

Begin working in rows.

Row 1: Ch 3, do **not** turn; 3 dc in same st as joining, 2 dc in each of next 7 dc, 4 dc in next dc, leave remaining 3 dc unworked: 22 dc.

Row 2: Ch 3, turn; hdc in first dc, sc in next 7 dc, hdc in next 6 dc, sc in next 7 dc, hdc in last dc; finish off leaving a long end for sewing.

Using photo, page 23, as a guide for placement and long ends, sew **wrong** side of Lily Pads and Lilies to **right** side of Blanket.

HAT

With Teal Ombre, ch 3; join with slip st to form a ring.

Rnd 1 (Right side)**:** Ch 3 **(does not count as a st, now and throughout)**, 12 dc in ring; skip beginning ch-3 **(now and throughout)** and join with slip st to first dc.

Rnd 2: Ch 3, 2 dc in same st as joining and in each dc around; join with slip st to first dc: 24 dc.

Rnd 3: Ch 3, dc in same st as joining, 2 dc in next dc, (dc in next dc, 2 dc in next dc) around; join with slip st to first dc: 36 dc.

Rnd 4: Ch 3, dc in same st as joining and in next dc, 2 dc in next dc, (dc in next 2 dc, 2 dc in next dc) around; join with slip st to first dc: 48 dc.

Rnd 5: Ch 3, dc in same st as joining and in next 2 dc, 2 dc in next dc, (dc in next 3 dc, 2 dc in next dc) around; join with slip st to first dc: 60 dc.

SIZE 0-6 MONTHS ONLY

Rnd 6: Ch 3, dc in same st as joining and in each dc around; join with slip st to first dc.

SIZE 6-12 MONTHS ONLY

Rnd 6: Ch 3, dc in same st as joining and in next 8 dc, 2 dc in next dc, (dc in next 9 dc, 2 dc in next dc) around; join with slip st to first dc: 66 dc.

Rnd 7: Ch 3, dc in same st as joining and in each dc around; join with slip st to first dc.

BOTH SIZES

Rnd 7{8}: Ch 3, dc in same st as joining and in each dc around, cut Teal Ombre; join with slip st to first dc changing to Green Ombre *(Fig. 5d, page 31)*.

Rnd 8{9}: Ch 3, dc in same st as joining and in each dc around; join with slip st to first dc.

Rnd 9{10}: Ch 3, dc in same st as joining and in each dc around, cut Green Ombre; join with slip st to first dc changing to Rose Ombre.

Last 2 Rnds: Ch 2 **(does not count as a st)**, hdc in same st as joining and in each st around; skip beginning ch-2 and join with slip st to first hdc.

Finish off.

Raindrops Set

EASY

SHOPPING LIST

Yarn (Medium Weight) 4

[3.5 ounces, 170 yards

(100 grams, 156 meters) per skein]:

- ☐ Rose - 2 skeins
- ☐ Blue - 2 skeins
- ☐ Dk Blue - 2 skeins
- ☐ White - 1 skein

Crochet Hook

- ☐ Size K (6.5 mm)

  or size needed for gauge

Additional Supplies

- ☐ Yarn needle

SIZE INFORMATION

BLANKET - 34½" wide x 27" long (87.5 cm x 68.5 cm)

HAT

Size: 0-6{6-12} Months

Fits Head Circumference:

13-15{16-17}"/33-38{40.5-43} cm

Size Note: We have printed the instructions for the Hat in different colors to make it easier for you to find:

- Size 0-6 Months in Blue
- Size 6-12 Months in Pink

Instructions in Black apply to both sizes.

GAUGE INFORMATION

In pattern,

12 sts and 10 rows/rnds = 4" (10 cm);

Gauge Swatch: 4¼" wide x 4" high (10.75 cm x 10 cm)

With Blue, ch 15.

Rows 1-10: Work same as Blanket Body through Row 4, then repeat Rows 3 and 4, 3 times: 13 sts.

Finish off.

STITCH GUIDE

SINGLE CROCHET 2 TOGETHER *(abbreviated sc2tog)*

Pull up a loop in each of next 2 sts, YO and draw through all 3 loops on hook **(counts as one sc)**.

FRONT POST TREBLE CROCHET *(abbreviated FPtr)*

YO twice, insert hook from **front** to **back** around post of dc one row or rnd **below** next sc *(Fig. 4, page 30)*, YO and pull up a loop (4 loops on hook), (YO and draw though 2 loops on hook) 3 times. Skip sc behind FPtr.

BLANKET

STRIPE SEQUENCE

5 Rows of Blue, ★ 4 rows of Dk Blue, 8 rows of Rose, 4 rows of Dk Blue, 4 rows of Blue; repeat from ★ throughout.

BODY

With Blue, ch 103; place marker in second ch from hook for Edging placement.

Row 1 (Right side)**:** Dc in fourth ch from hook **(3 skipped chs count as first dc)** and in each ch across: 101 dc.

Note: Loop a short piece of yarn around any stitch to mark Row 1 as **right** side.

Row 2: Ch 1, turn; sc in each st across.

Row 3: Ch 3 **(counts as first dc, now and throughout)**, turn; ★ work FPtr around dc one row **below** next sc, dc in next sc; repeat from ★ across: 51 dc and 50 FPtr.

Row 4: Ch 1, turn; sc in each st across: 101 sc.

Row 5: Ch 3, turn; ★ dc in next sc, work FPtr around dc one row **below** next sc; repeat from ★ across to last 2 sc, dc in last 2 sc changing to next color in last dc made *(Fig. 5c, page 31)*: 52 dc and 49 FPtr.

Rows 6-64: Continuing to follow Stripe Sequence, repeat Rows 2-5, 14 times; then repeat Rows 2-4 once **more**: 101 sc.

Row 65: Ch 3, turn; ★ dc in next sc, work FPtr around dc one row **below** next sc; repeat from ★ across to last 2 sc, dc in last 2 sc changing to White in last dc made: 52 dc and 49 FPtr.

EDGING

Rnd 1: Ch 1, do **not** turn; † working in ends of rows, sc in first 2 rows, 2 sc in next row, (sc in next row, 2 sc in next row) across, ch 2 †; working in free loops of beginning ch *(Fig. 3, page 30)*, sc2tog, sc in each ch across ending in marked ch, ch 2; repeat from † to † once; working in sts across Row 65, sc2tog, sc in each st across, ch 2; join with slip st to first sc: 394 sc and 8 chs.

Rnd 2: Ch 1, (sc, ch 2, sc) in same st as joining, skip next 2 sc, ★ (sc, ch 2, sc) in next st, skip next 2 sts; repeat from ★ around; join with slip st to first sc, finish off.

CLOUD (Make 4)

With White, ch 8.

Rnd 1 (Right side)**:** 2 Dc in fourth ch from hook **(3 skipped chs count as first dc)**, dc in next 3 chs, 6 dc in last ch; working in free loops of beginning ch, dc in next 3 chs, 3 dc in next ch; join with slip st to first dc: 18 dc.

Note: Mark Rnd 1 as **right** side.

Rnd 2: Ch 1, sc in same st as joining, skip next dc, 5 dc in next dc, skip next dc, sc in next dc, 5 hdc in next dc, sc in next dc, skip next dc, 10 dc in next dc, skip next dc, sc in next dc, skip next dc, 6 dc in next dc, skip next dc, sc in next dc, skip next dc, 6 hdc in next dc, sc in next dc, 3 dc in same st as first sc; join with slip st to first sc, finish off leaving a long end for sewing.

Thread yarn needle with long end and sew **wrong** side of one Cloud to **right** side of each corner of Blanket.

HAT

With Blue, ch 3; join with slip st to form a ring.

Rnd 1 (Right side)**:** Ch 3 (**does not count as a st, now and throughout**), 12 dc in ring; skip beginning ch-3 (**now and throughout**) and join with slip st to first dc.

Rnd 2: Ch 3, 2 dc in same st as joining and in each dc around; join with slip st to first dc: 24 dc.

Rnd 3: Ch 3, dc in same st as joining, 2 dc in next dc, (dc in next dc, 2 dc in next dc) around; join with slip st to first dc: 36 dc.

Rnd 4: Ch 3, dc in same st as joining and in next 4{1} dc, 2 dc in next dc, ★ dc in next 5{2} dc, 2 dc in next dc; repeat from ★ around; join with slip st to first dc: 42{48} dc.

Size 0-6 Months ONLY

Rnd 5: Ch 3, dc in same st as joining and in each dc around, cut Blue; join with slip st to first dc changing to Dk Blue *(Fig. 5d, page 31)*.

SIZE 6-12 MONTHS ONLY

Rnd 5: Ch 3, dc in same st as joining and in each dc around; join with slip st to first dc.

Rnd 6: Ch 3, dc in same st as joining and in each dc around, cut Blue; join with slip st to first dc changing to Dk Blue *(Fig. 5d, page 31)*.

BOTH SIZES

Rnd 6{7}: Ch 1, **turn**; sc in each dc around; join with slip st to first sc.

Rnd 7{8}: Ch 3, turn; dc in first sc, work FPtr around dc one rnd **below** next sc, ★ dc in next sc, work FPtr around dc one rnd **below** next sc; repeat from ★ around; join with slip st to first dc: 21{24} dc and 21{24} FPtr.

Rnd 8{9}: Ch 1, turn; sc in each st around; join with slip st to first sc: 42{48} sc.

Rnd 9{10}: Ch 3, turn; work FPtr around dc one rnd **below** first sc, dc in next dc, ★ work FPtr around dc one rnd **below** next sc, dc in next dc; repeat from ★ around, cut Dk Blue; join with slip st to first dc changing to Rose: 21{24} dc and 21{24} FPtr.

Next 2 Rnds: Repeat Rnds 6{7} and 7{8}: 21{24} dc and 21{24} FPtr.

Last Rnd: Ch 1, turn; sc in each st around, cut Rose; join with slip st to first dc changing to White: 42{48} sc.

Trim: Ch 1, turn; (sc, ch 2, sc) in first sc, skip next 2 sc, ★ (sc, ch 2, sc) in next sc, skip next 2 sc; repeat from ★ around; join with slip st to first sc, finish off.

General Instructions

ABBREVIATIONS

ch(s)	chain(s)
cm	centimeters
dc	double crochet(s)
dc2tog	double crochet 2 together
FPtr	Front Post treble crochet(s)
hdc	half double crochet(s)
mm	millimeters
Rnd(s)	Round(s)
sc	single crochet(s)
sc2tog	single crochet 2 together
sc3tog	single crochet 3 together
sp(s)	space(s)
st(s)	stitch(es)
tr	treble crochet(s)
tr2tog	treble crochet 2 together
tr3tog	treble crochet 3 together
YO	yarn over

SYMBOLS & TERMS

★ — work instructions following ★ as many **more** times as indicated in addition to the first time.

† to † **or** ♥ to ♥ — work all instructions from first † to second † **or** from first ♥ to second ♥ **as many** times as specified.

( ) or [ ] — work enclosed instructions **as many** times as specified by the number immediately following **or** work all enclosed instructions in the stitch or space indicated **or** contains explanatory remarks.

colon (:) — the number(s) given after a colon at the end of a row or round denote(s) the number of stitches or spaces you should have on that row or round.

GAUGE

Exact gauge is **essential** for proper size. Before beginning your project, make the sample swatch given in the individual instructions in the yarn and hook specified. After completing the swatch, measure it, counting your stitches and rows or rounds carefully. If your swatch is larger or smaller than specified, **make another, changing hook size to get the correct gauge**. Keep trying until you find the size hook that will give you the specified gauge.

CROCHET TERMINOLOGY		
UNITED STATES		INTERNATIONAL
slip stitch (slip st)	=	single crochet (sc)
single crochet (sc)	=	double crochet (dc)
half double crochet (hdc)	=	half treble crochet (htr)
double crochet (dc)	=	treble crochet (tr)
treble crochet (tr)	=	double treble crochet (dtr)
double treble crochet (dtr)	=	triple treble crochet (ttr)
triple treble crochet (tr tr)	=	quadruple treble crochet (qtr)
skip	=	miss

BEGINNER	Projects for first-time crocheters using basic stitches. Minimal shaping.
EASY	Projects using yarn with basic stitches, repetitive stitch patterns, simple color changes, and simple shaping and finishing.
INTERMEDIATE	Projects using a variety of techniques, such as basic lace patterns or color patterns, mid-level shaping and finishing.
EXPERIENCED	Projects with intricate stitch patterns, techniques and dimension, such as non-repeating patterns, multi-color techniques, fine threads, small hooks, detailed shaping and refined finishing.

CROCHET HOOKS

U.S.	B-1	C-2	D-3	E-4	F-5	G-6	7	H-8	I-9	J-10	K-10½	L-11	M/N-13	N/P-15	P/Q	Q	S
Metric - mm	2.25	2.75	3.25	3.5	3.75	4	4.5	5	5.5	6	6.5	8	9	10	15	16	19

JOINING WITH SC

When instructed to join with sc, begin with a slip knot on hook. Insert hook in stitch indicated, YO and pull up a loop, YO and draw through both loops on hook.

JOINING WITH HDC

When instructed to join with hdc, begin with a slip knot on hook. YO, holding loop on hook, insert hook in stitch or space indicated, YO and pull up a loop (3 loops on hook), YO and draw through all 3 loops on hook.

JOINING WITH DC

When instructed to join with dc, begin with a slip knot on hook. YO, holding loop on hook, insert hook in stitch or space indicated, YO and pull up a loop (3 loops on hook), (YO and draw through 2 loops on hook) twice.

BACK RIDGE

Work only in loops indicated by arrows ***(Fig. 1)***.

Fig. 1

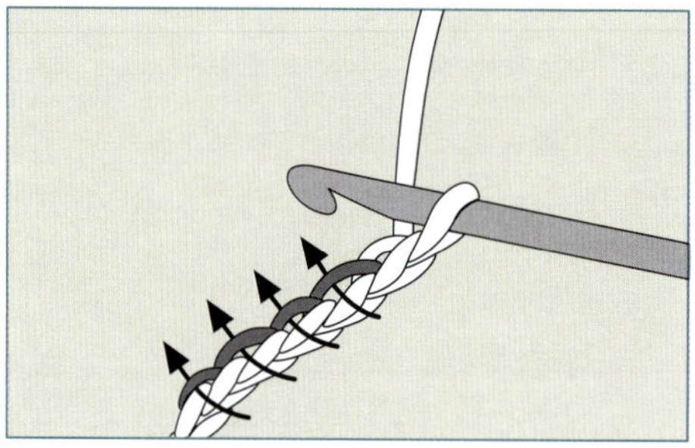

BACK LOOPS ONLY

Work only in loop(s) indicated by arrows ***(Fig. 2)***.

Fig. 2

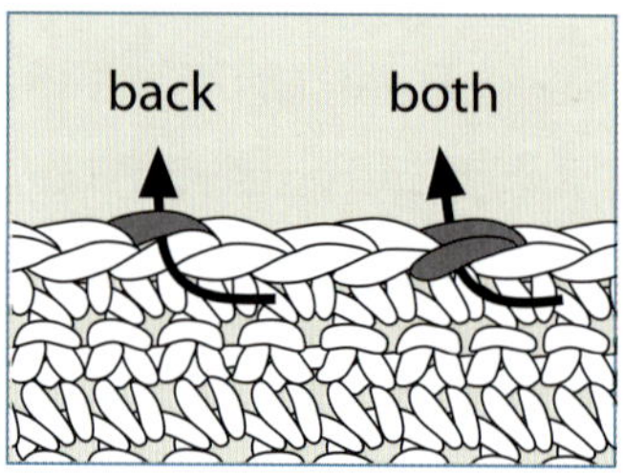

FREE LOOPS OF A CHAIN

When instructed to work in free loops of a chain, work in loops indicated by arrow ***(Fig. 3)***.

Fig. 3

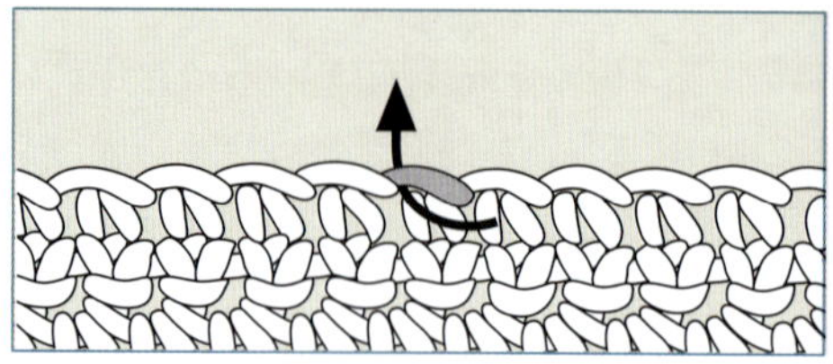

FRONT POST STITCH

Work around the post of the stitch indicated, inserting the hook in the direction of the arrow ***(Fig. 4)***.

Fig. 4

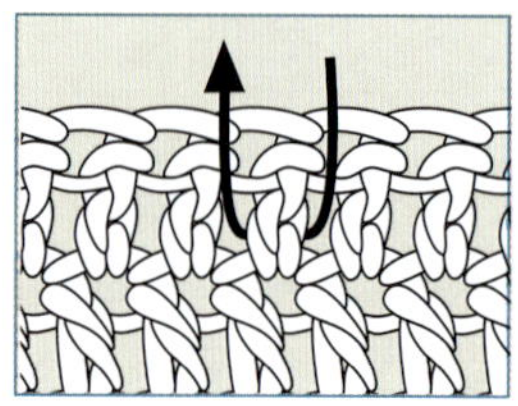

Yarn Weight Symbol & Names	LACE 0	SUPER FINE 1	FINE 2	LIGHT 3	MEDIUM 4	BULKY 5	SUPER BULKY 6	JUMBO 7
Type of Yarns in Category	Fingering, size 10 crochet thread	Sock, Fingering, Baby	Sport, Baby	DK, Light Worsted	Worsted, Afghan, Aran	Chunky, Craft, Rug	Super Bulky, Roving	Jumbo, Roving
Crochet Gauge* Ranges in Single Crochet to 4" (10 cm)	32-42 sts**	21-32 sts	16-20 sts	12-17 sts	11-14 sts	8-11 sts	6-9 sts	5 sts and fewer
Advised Hook Size Range	Steel*** 6 to 8, Regular hook B-1	B-1 to E-4	E-4 to 7	7 to I-9	I-9 to K-10½	K-10½ to M/N-13	M/N-13 to Q	Q and larger

*GUIDELINES ONLY: The chart above reflects the most commonly used gauges and hook sizes for specific yarn categories.

** Lace weight yarns are usually crocheted with larger hooks to create lacy openwork patterns. Accordingly, a gauge range is difficult to determine. Always follow the gauge stated in your pattern.

*** Steel crochet hooks are sized differently from regular hooks–the higher the number, the smaller the hook, which is the reverse of regular hook sizing.

CHANGING COLORS

Work the last stitch to within one step of completion, drop yarn, hook new yarn ***(Figs. 5a, b, c, or d)*** and draw through all loops on hook. Do **not** cut old color unless indicated.

Fig. 5a

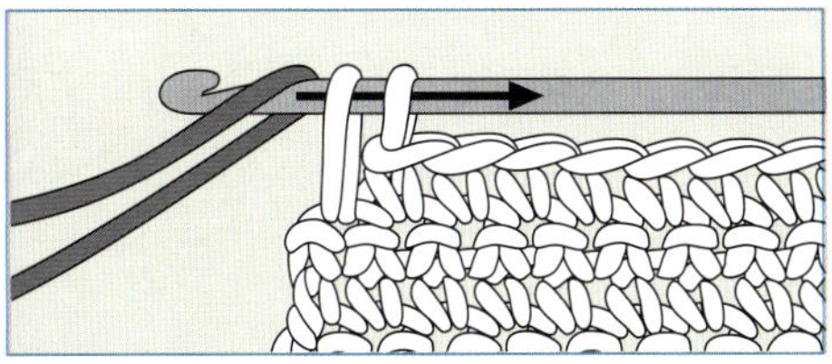

Fig. 5b

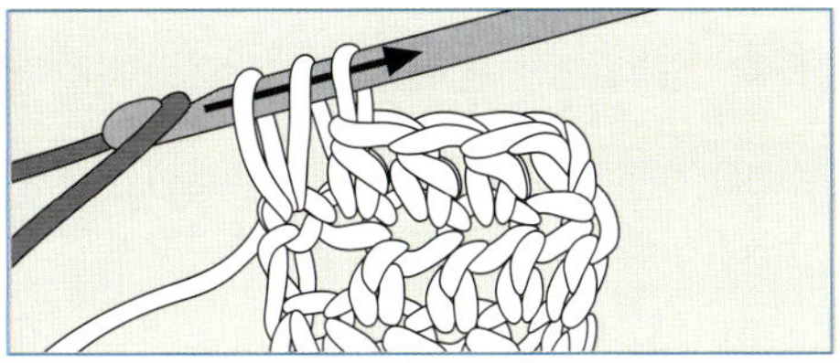

Fig. 5c

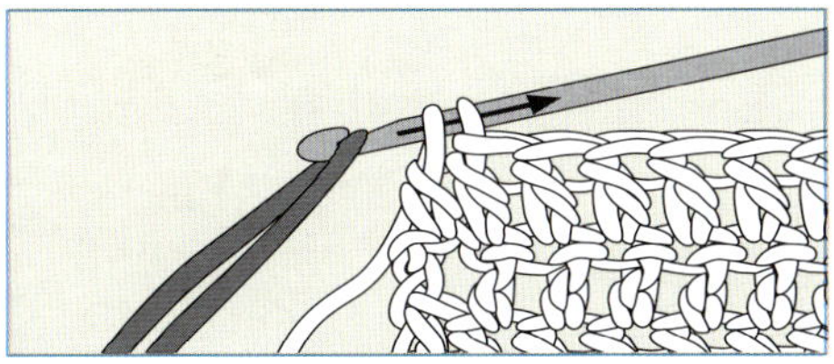

Fig. 5d

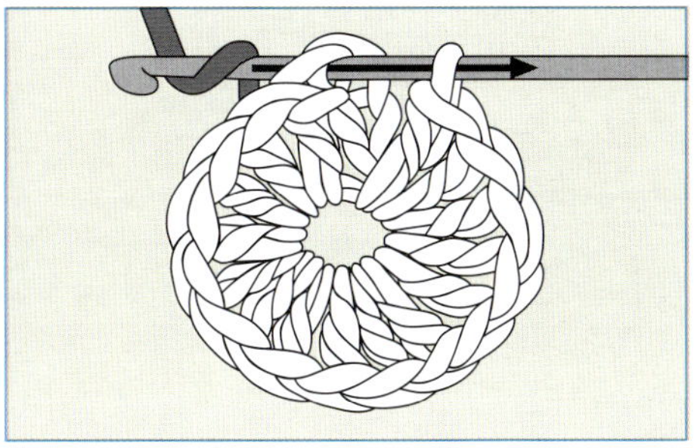

Meet Sara Leighton

Sara Leighton is a passionate crochet designer and blogger who is most inspired by the universe, nature, science, city life in Seattle, and color.

"The beauty and complexity of nature has inspired artists and craftspeople throughout history. What better way to celebrate nature's most precious gift, a new life, than to create special handmade items influenced by the amazing plants, animals, and elements in the world around us," she says.

"My first experience with crochet was receiving a beloved crochet chevron blanket from my grandmother when I was a young child. Upon learning to crochet in college, I began to intimately appreciate her hard work. Crochet is now my favorite way to bring beautiful things into the world and to connect with other passionate crafters. It's amazing how all of those little stitches come together to make a complete object."

Originally from Boise, Idaho, Sara has a Bachelor's degree in Psychology and a Master's degree in Teaching. She loves the excitement of living in Seattle, Washington, with many friends and a sweet little cream cat named Ranna to keep her company.

"When I'm not crocheting, I'm teaching, singing karaoke, quilling, reading, and baking/cooking. I meet with the Rainy Sunday Knitters every week for fiber fun of all kinds. My favorite food is popcorn and my favorite color is purple. I collect perfumes, antique keys, glass bottles, and jewelry."

For more about Sara, visit illuminatecrochet.blogspot.com or find her on Ravelry, Craftsy, Facebook, Instagram, and Pinterest.

Yarn Information

The projects in this book were made using a variety of yarn weights. Any brand of the specified weight of yarn may be used. It is best to refer to the yardage/meters when determining how many balls or skeins to purchase. Remember, to arrive at the finished size, it is the GAUGE/TENSION that is important, not the brand of yarn.

For your convenience, listed below are specific yarns used to create our photography models. Because yarn manufacturers make frequent changes in their product lines, you may sometimes find it necessary to use a substitute yarn or to search for the discontinued product at alternate suppliers (locally or online).

CONIFEROUS SET

Bernat® Super Value™

Green - #53243 Forest Green

Brown - #53015 Taupe Heather

Dk Green - #07759 Deep Sea Green

Dk Brown - #53013 Chocolate

STARRY SET

Red Heart® Soft®

Navy - #4604 Navy

Off White - #4601 Off White

FOX SET

Lion Brand® Wool-Ease® Thick & Quick®

Brown - #501 Sequoia

Beige - #098 Linen

Orange - #136 Apricot

SEEDLING SET

Red Heart® With Love®

Aran - #1303 Aran

Brown - #1321 Chocolate

Green - #1601 Lettuce

SUNRISE SET

Caron® Simply Soft®

Red - #9730 Autumn Red

Orange - #9765 Pumpkin

Yellow - #9755 Sunshine

WATER LILIES SET

Caron® Simple Soft® Ombre™

Teal Ombre - #08701 Teal Zeal

Green Ombre - #08243 Avocado

Rose Ombre - #08434 Rosewood

RAINDROPS SET

Lion Brand® Vanna's Choice®

Rose - #143 Antique Rose

Blue - #105 Silver Blue

Dk Blue - #109 Colonial Blue

White - #100 White

We have made every effort to ensure that these instructions are accurate and complete. We cannot, however, be responsible for human error, typographical mistakes, or variations in individual work.

Production Team: Technical Writer/Editor - Lois J. Long; Editorial Writer - Susan Frantz Wiles; Senior Graphic Artist - Lora Puls; Graphic Artists - Frances Huddleston and Victoria Temple; Photo Stylist - Sondra Daniel; and Photographer - Ken West.